Help I'm Creating A Small Business

By
Jasmine Baker

Copyrights Notice

No part of this book can be transmitted or reproduced in any form including print, electronic, photocopying, scanning, mechanical, or recording without prior written permission from the author.

All information, ideas, and guidelines presented here are for educational purposes only. This book cannot be used to replace information provided with the device. All readers are encouraged to seek professional advice when needed.

While the author has taken utmost efforts to ensure the accuracy of the written content, all readers are advised to follow the information mentioned herein at their own risk. The author cannot be held responsible for any personal or commercial damage caused by misinterpretation of information or improper use of the information.

Legal Notice

The Publisher has strived to be as accurate and complete as possible in the creation of this report, notwithstanding the fact that he does not warrant or represent at any time that the contents within are accurate due to the rapidly changing nature of the Internet.

The Publisher will not be responsible for any losses or damages of any kind incurred by the reader whether directly or indirectly arising from the use of the information found in this report.

This report is not intended for use as a source of legal, business, accounting or financial advice. All readers are advised to seek services of competent professionals in legal, business, accounting, and finance field.

No guarantees of success and/or income are made. Reader assumes responsibility for use of information contained herein. The author reserves the right to make changes without notice. The Publisher assumes no responsibility or liability whatsoever on the behalf of the reader of this report.

Table of Contents

Introduction 1

Chapter One - Why A Small Business? 2

    The Benefits of Starting a Small Side Business 2

    What Is the Failure Rate of Small Businesses? 5

    Why Do Small Businesses Fail? 7

    The Growth of Small Businesses 8

    The State of Small Businesses Pre-and-Post COVID-19 11

    Resources 16

Chapter Two - Talking About Small Business 17

    Small Business Pros during the Pandemic 17

    Small Business Cons during the Pandemic 21

    How to achieve financial freedom with a successful small business 24

    Resources 27

Chapter Three – Business Location - Brick and Mortar VS Online 29

    The Brick and Mortar Business 30

    Online Businesses 31

    Internet Enterprise vs. Traditional Enterprise 32

    Resources 34

Chapter Four - Business Name Selection 35

    STEP 1: DEVELOPING A BUSINESS NAME: 36

    STEP 2: SEARCH FOR DUPLICATE NAMES: 40

    STEP 3: CHECKING A GOVERNMENT DATABASE FOR TRADEMARKS 43

    Resources 44

Chapter Five - Small Business Essentials 45

    How to Pick the Right Legal Structure for Your Business 45

    Resources 61

Chapter six - Business Plan the Secret Weapon! 62

    Planning for business success 62

    Budgeting and planning in business: 63

    Budgeting and strategic planning 64

    The advantages of a business budget 65

    What exactly is business capital, and why is it so crucial? 66

    What is the formula for business capital? 66

    There are four reasons why your business could need more
operating capital. 68

    Looking for ways to increase your business capital? 68

    What is the significance of business accounting? 69

    What Is the Importance of Accounting? 70

    The Importance of Filing a Business Income Tax Return 72

    The Importance of POS (Point-of-Sale) Systems for Small
Businesses 75

    Resources 78

Chapter Seven - Understanding Your Industry Competitors 79

    How to Conduct a Market Analysis for Your Business 79

    What is the definition of a market analysis? 80

    What are the advantages of conducting a marketing study? 81

    What is the best way to perform a market analysis? 83

    Resources 86

Conclusion 87

Introduction

Making the decision to start a business can be one of the most exciting decisions you'll ever make. We live in a world where everyone is looking for ways to supplement their income. The majority of people have done so through getting amazing company concepts. When starting a business, one must be prepared to face competition. It is vital to highlight that in order to succeed in business, you do not need to be wealthy or well-known; instead, you must think strategically. However, there are numerous moving pieces and variables to consider.

Many people are drawn to the concept of entrepreneurship, but figuring out how to get started can be intimidating. What should you put on the market? Who should you offer your product to? What strategy will you use to attract customers?

Making the decision to establish your own business is a big step. It necessitates stepping outside of your comfort zone and attempting something new. Why wait if that concept fascinates you? You're ready to take the plunge and start your own business. It takes a lot of time and effort, and there are certain risks involved, but the potential for rewards is enormous.

Stop overthinking and start doing the effort to make it happen if you're serious about launching a business.

We'll walk you through the process of starting a small business in 2021 in this guide.

Chapter One - Why A Small Business?

Entrepreneurial opportunities, jobs for neighbors, and gathering places for communities are all provided by small enterprises. They're embedded in the environment in which they flourish, and they return vigor and nourishment. Despite the fact that owning a small business entails taking more risks than working for a large, established corporation, the benefits are both quantitative and qualitative, including widespread wealth and a network of symbiotic ties.

Developing a business idea and launching a company can seem daunting and hard. There are numerous factors to consider, ranging from coming up with a great concept to forming a business, to business planning, fundraising, and much more.

The Benefits of Starting a Small Side Business

Entrepreneurship is a word that I both admire and loathe. The thought of turning a beginning business into a large corporation excites me as someone who aspires to one day launch a great company. Others might pass up my fantasy in favor of steady work that pays the bills. Neither approach is superior to the other. It all relies on one's personal goals in life.

So, why are so many internet entrepreneurs crying from the rooftops about how it's a waste of time to work a 9-to-5 job and instead start a business full-time? Not only is that an overgeneralization, but it's also a restricting worldview. Elon Musk, Mark Zuckerberg, and Reid Hoffman are hardly the only ones who have succeeded as entrepreneurs. With a tiny side business, you can easily flex your entrepreneurial muscles while working full-time. In fact, I strongly advise you to try it at least once. It will not only be a great experience, but it will also provide numerous benefits that will aid you in your current or future work.

1. Tax Advantages

Many purchases, including home office space, office supplies, furniture, and even business miles driven, can be deducted as business costs. If you despise giving over your hard-earned money to Uncle Sam (and I haven't met anyone who doesn't!), you should create your LLC as soon as possible.

2. Additional Revenue Stream

The average revenue of a "non-employer" (one-person) business is more than $40,000 per year. Even if you only made $10,000 in profit, it would put more than $300 in your pocket each month. Also, keep in mind that $10,000 is the average, not the maximum. Nothing is keeping your company from bringing in a lot more money. What would you do if you had an extra $300, $600, or even $1000 per month?

3. Increased Control

The average millionaire has seven different sources of income. If one goes missing, the millionaire has six more to fall back on. A side business provides you with a second source of income, which not only increases your income but also allows you more control over your life. Your job no longer owns you, according to the second revenue stream. You have the option of quitting your work and growing your business. When your supervisor doesn't grant you that increase, you won't be (too) disappointed. You won't be upset if your slacker coworker is promoted ahead of you. Why? Because your job isn't everything to you. You're running a business from home that pays you hundreds, if not thousands, of dollars per month.

4. Work Experience to Complement Your Curriculum Vitae

If your side business is a success, you can include it on your resume as experience. This might easily set you apart from other applicants who only have an MBA or basic management experience. Personally, I'd rather hire a Harvard MBA with no experience than a high school dropout with real business expertise and success.

5. Increased Happiness

When it comes to satisfaction, company owners outnumber workers by 77 percent, whereas 52 percent of Americans are dissatisfied with their occupations. If you're one of the 48% who enjoys their job, take use of the advantages of both being an employee and a business owner. If you despise your job, starting a side business is a great way to get away from it all and possibly replace it. Take a chance; there's nothing to lose.

To become an entrepreneur, you don't have to establish a cutting-edge tech company. Running a business while working full-time is not only possible, but also advantageous. I've previously highlighted the advantages. You must now go to the next stage. Whatever it takes to start your own small side business and enjoy the control and independence it provides.

What Is the Failure Rate of Small Businesses?

Small firms fail 20% of the time in their first year, 30% of the time in their second year, and 50% of the time in their fifth year. Finally, 70% of small business entrepreneurs fail within the first ten years of operation.

There's a lot of uncertainty ahead of you as a new entrepreneur getting ready to start a firm or as a business owner who's just opened their doors. Everyone you've told about your idea has most likely highlighted (very unhelpfully) the percentage of small firms that fail.

You have every right to be concerned, whether they have provided you accurate or incorrect statistics. After all, starting a small business is a significant risk—you never know how your product will change, if you'll qualify for a small business loan, or if you'll even survive the many problems that come with running a small business.

Because many small firms flourish, it's useful to know what percentage of them fail. And you don't want someone to jolt you awake from your slumber. Having facts is the finest thing you can do.

Let's go over this information, as well as some other important small business facts.

What Is the Failure Rate of Small Businesses?

According to data from the Bureau of Labor Statistics, roughly 20% of small firms fail in their first year, and over 50% of small businesses fail in their fifth year. However, viewing this figure in terms of how many American small enterprises survive is also instructive. Here's what the survival rate looks like, according to the Bureau of Labor Statistics' Business Employment Dynamics:

- Approximately 80% of enterprises with employees will survive their first year.
- Around 70% of enterprises with employees will make it through their second year.
- About half of all enterprises with employees will make it to their fifth year.
- Only about a third of enterprises will make it to their tenth year.

However, the quotable statistic you require is that approximately 20% of small enterprises fail in their first year, and 50% fail in their fifth year.

These rates have remained constant over time. Surprisingly, this implies that year-over-year economic considerations have little impact on how many small enterprises survive in the United States. The message here is that you can pretty much count on an 80%, 70%, 50%, and 30% survival percentage after one, two, five, and ten years in a company, regardless of the year.

It's vital to clarify that this statistic applies to all private-sector enterprises. While the overall survival statistics for small firms are fairly consistent, the facts differ when looking at business failure by industry.

Why Do Small Businesses Fail?

The four most prevalent reasons for small businesses failing, according to Investopedia, are a lack of sufficient cash, poor management, and inadequate company planning, and overspending on marketing.

Cash Flow Issues However, there are many more reasons why early-stage enterprises in this country fail.

According to the founders of 101 startups polled by CBInsights, there are a variety of reasons why they failed. The top outcomes were as follows:

- Because there is no market demand for their services or products, 42% of small firms fail.
- Due to a lack of funds, 29% of the participants failed.
- Because they didn't have the right staff to run the business, 23% of them failed.
- Outcompeted 19% of the time.
- Pricing and cost difficulties accounted for 18% of the failures.
- 17% of businesses failed due to a poor product offering.
- Because they lacked a business concept, 17% of them failed.
- 14% of businesses failed due to poor marketing.
- Customers were ignored by 14% of those who failed.

There are numerous reasons why small businesses fail, but a few stand out: lack of money, cash flow, lack of demand, and poor management.

The Growth of Small Businesses

If you look at the percentage of small enterprises that fail, the US small company sector may appear to be absolutely doomed. However, a slew of other figures demonstrate that small companies in the United States are thriving. So, if you're having second thoughts about starting a small business, remember these five facts.

1. Small enterprises run by women are thriving and increasing.

According to American express research, female entrepreneurship increased by 114% between 1997 and 2017.

We still have a long way to go before we achieve gender equality in the entrepreneurial world, but the fact that women-owned businesses regularly outlast male-owned businesses indicates the resilience and perseverance of female entrepreneurs.

More excellent news: women own more than 11.6 million businesses in the United States. These businesses employ approximately 9 million people and earned $1.7 trillion in revenue in 2017. For female small company entrepreneurs, things are looking up.

2. The number of minority-owned small businesses is growing.

There is also some good news for minority-owned small companies. The number of minority-owned businesses in the United States increased by 38% between 2007 and 2016, according to research by the Minority Business Development Agency.

Between 2007 and 2012, the number of African-American-owned businesses in the United States increased by 34%. During those years, the number of Hispanic-owned firms in the United States increased by 46%.

Again, there is still room for these figures to rise, but greater diversity among small company owners in the United States is positive.

3. Small enterprises account for a large portion of the economy.

You can be proud as a small business owner that you and your fellow entrepreneurs make up the majority of the economy. There is a wealth of data that shows how important small enterprises are in the United States.

Small enterprises in the United States include:
- 99.9% of all businesses in the country.
- 99.7% of all businesses with paid staff.
- 97.7% of all exporting companies are
- Employees in the private sector make up 48% of the workforce.
- 41.2% of the workforce is employed in the private sector.
- 33.6% of the total value of known exports

The economy of the United States is dominated by small businesses. If you're having a bad day at work, keep these numbers in mind.

4. Small firms are responsible for the majority of job growth in the United States.

If you operate a business and manage staff, you're part of the reason behind these incredible job creation figures:

Small businesses employed 56.8 million people in 2013, accounting for 48% of the private workforce.

Small firms added 1.4 million new jobs in the first three fiscal quarters of 2014, with very small enterprises accounting for 39% of the total (with fewer than 50 employees).

Small businesses account for 63% of net new job creation in the United States.

5. Small firms are opening at a faster rate than they are closing.

Finally, certain small company figures reveal a bright spot in the market: small firms are opening at a quicker rate than they are closing for the first time since the recession.

This is also good news for employment creation in the United States. According to recent research, one-third of the 16,000 small businesses polled grew their personnel in 2016, and a whopping 60% of all organizations predicted an increase in income that year.

The bottom line is that small businesses make up the great majority of businesses in the United States. Overall, the number of small enterprises opening their doors is increasing. Women's and minority-owned small companies, in particular, have recently surged in number.

Small Business Survival Rates in the Big Picture

When you stand back from this small business data and consider the larger picture, the major conclusion is that running a small business is difficult, as seen by the high percentage of small enterprises that fail. There are a variety of reasons why small businesses fail, but in general, keep an eye on your capital sources and cash flow—these are often the deciding factors in whether or not a firm will succeed.

But small company owners keep your chin up. Small company owners are becoming more optimistic, and the strength of small enterprises in the US economy is being reinforced by incredible numbers year after year.

The State of Small Businesses Pre-and-Post COVID-19

COVID-19 had a tremendous influence on various industries in the United States, with many businesses suffering financial losses as a result. According to a survey from Intuit QuickBooks, small companies (SMBs) were among the hardest hit, losing a total of $4.6 billion in monthly sales in April 2020 alone. SMBs' financial health had collapsed by 2020, when the epidemic was at its peak.

Now, in 2021, we are passed the pandemic, the economy is beginning to recover, and businesses are eager to rebound from the problems of the previous year. According to data from Intuit QuickBooks, SMBs in fields including finance and agriculture have experienced significant growth since the pandemic's peak. Even some of the most hard-hit industries are starting to recover. So, what does this mean for small and medium-sized businesses in the oil and gas industry? Luke Voiles, Intuit's VP and General Manager of QuickBooks Capital, discusses the present state of the oil and gas industry, how oil and gas SMBs are rebounding in comparison to other SMBs, and what SMBs should do to continue company growth in the future.

According to the Intuit QuickBooks research, the oil and gas industry was one of the most hit, with sales dropping by more than 20% - the equivalent of more than $80,000 per company. Despite the fact that oil and gas were regarded critical industries, oil prices plummeted during the pandemic, as is typical of a downturn, according to Voiles. "I don't believe anyone could have imagined the worldwide lockdowns that followed the pandemic's formal declaration in February 2020. People were unable to travel, and supply and demand for many goods and services were interrupted, while demand for others increased."

Halliburton

Despite being among the hardest hit, the oil and gas industry is steadily recovering. "Our data suggests that the oil and gas industry is rebounding as more enterprises open up and individuals begin to travel again, now that vaccine rollouts are underway," says Voiles. Monthly revenues for small enterprises in the industry have been steadily increasing since last summer's low point, and many are now close to pre-pandemic levels, which are encouraging." However, despite this upward trend, SMBs may still face difficulties. One of the obstacles, according to Voiles, could be the rise in demand. "We'll be keeping a careful eye on the statistics from May and June," Voiles says.

Oil and gas is improving dramatically in compared to other industries. "According to the most recent data, monthly revenues for small enterprises in the oil and gas industry are at 90% of pre-pandemic levels through April 2021. "This is a huge improvement over the low point in July 2020, when monthly revenues were only 65% of pre-pandemic levels," Voiles notes. He also presented information on the recovery of other industries that had been severely impacted by the pandemic. Hotels' monthly income dropped by 48 percent in April 2020, but was up about 12 percent in March 2021 compared to pre-pandemic levels. Education, which was hit harder than oil and gas in April 2020, had a two-percent increase in monthly income in March 2021 compared to before the epidemic.

Many SMBs are recovering and enjoying revenue improvements now that the economy is open again. Businesses may find themselves in difficulty if things go wrong and the economy shuts down again. Voiles emphasize the need of understanding your company's cash flow in order to overcome hurdles such as closures and regulations.

"When things are tough, money and cash flow become unavoidable concerns. If left uncontrolled, [they] have the potential to spiral out of control. Look for financial solutions that give you a speedier method to get paid, a simpler way to pay your payments, an easy way to access new sources of capital, and the most comprehensive means to understand and control your cash flow into the future to help you stabilize your cash flow," Voiles recommends.

Cash reserves, according to Voiles, can be a valuable financial option for business owners, particularly in the event of a pandemic. "The old adage of having three to six months' worth of cash reserves appears to be a remnant from another era. Set a long-term goal of conserving enough money to keep your firm running for a year and include it in your business plan. We advocate researching digital technology options to assist your firm establish resilience, in addition to correctly managing your financial flow," Voiles says. Small businesses who invested in digital technology in 2020 fared better during the pandemic and were more confidence about the future, according to a survey by Intuit QuickBooks.

What are the next measures for SMBs now that they are on the mend? Small business owners and employees, according to Voiles, should take time to process everything that has happened in the previous year. "Reflect on what worked and what didn't throughout this tough period. "Make sure you have a well-thought-out company plan that will enable you to respond to unforeseen circumstances," Voiles advises. He points out that more than one out of every ten prospective business owners does not intend to prepare a business plan, despite the fact that 69 percent of small business owners believe this is a mistake. Writing a business strategy can benefit both new and established businesses.

SMB owners should also concentrate on their financial strategy, according to Voiles. "Will your funds be in order if you run into unexpected difficulties in the future and require emergency assistance, so you can request for relief quickly?" It's also a good opportunity to make sure you're not unduly reliant on a single source of income. Diversify your business as much as possible, and embrace technology to create new ways to reach customers," Voiles advises.

As a result of COVID-19, QuickBooks has been assisting small businesses who have had to immediately adapt their business practices with little to no direction. "By becoming an approved PPP lender, generating and sharing resources, and co-founding The Small Business Relief Initiative with GoFundMe, we were one of the first companies to aid small businesses. Last year, QuickBooks Capital assisted qualifying customers in obtaining more than $1.2 billion in SBA-approved loans and Paycheck Protection Program (PPP) support through the CARES Act," says Voiles.

In the event that a similar circumstance arises again, Voiles and QuickBooks have been vociferous in demanding that the government do more for small businesses. "We're striving to make the COVID-19 relief fund more accessible, to provide government support for small businesses, and to make it easier for small firms to go digital. "You can learn more about this effort in our Small Business Recovery Report's "Why this Matters" section," says Voiles.

So, what does the future hold for SMBs in general and SMBs in the oil and gas business in particular? With data demonstrating the tenacity of many small businesses, the road to recovery appears to be clear. "While certain industries have taken longer to recover, most are now back to pre-pandemic levels," adds Voiles. Though the oil and gas industry has progressed, Voiles points out that it still lags behind other industries, particularly those that were more robust to the pandemic, like as real estate and agriculture. "It's critical that we keep an eye on the data in the coming months and acknowledge that some enterprises may still require more assistance."

Resources

For making your own logo, LogoGarden is a fantastic free alternative. This is for you if you want something simple, do-it-yourself, and free.

Fiverr, like 99designs, is a marketplace for designers, copywriters, programmers, and other professionals.

Shopify distinguishes itself from other website builders by focusing on online sales. Shopify isn't for you if you don't need to sell online and only require a "brochure" webpage.

Zoom Meetings — A streamlined video conferencing and messaging service, Zoom Meetings allows you to video conference, message, and share content.

Hootsuite - Hootsuite is a free social media management tool that allows you to post to numerous channels at once.

WordPress began as a blogging tool, but it has evolved into much more.

Weebly — Owned by Square, Weebly caters to a wide range of consumers with simple and advanced functionality.

Chapter Two - Talking About Small Business

The continuous COVID-19 pandemic has wreaked havoc on the business world, affecting small enterprises, corporations, and franchisees alike. Here are small business pros and cons during the pandemic:

Small Business Pros during the Pandemic

COVID-19 has given new significance to perks that may have previously been overlooked by employees.

With benefits and tools, more firms are assisting their employees in navigating financial issues, both individually and as a family.

Employees and employers alike recognize the need for coverage that protects the health and well-being of both individuals and their families, and COVID-19 has profoundly transformed the benefits market. This has highlighted the importance of benefits in attracting and maintaining top personnel among employers, particularly among small businesses.

Despite rising unemployment rates, many business owners still struggle to find and keep top employees. According to a recent NFIB report, finding competent personnel is second only to the expense of health care. Finding methods to engage with employees and matching benefits offers with their beliefs and goals will be crucial as small firms plan for the future.

New types of benefits are becoming available.

Benefits that may have previously ranked lower on an employee's priority list, such as income protection resources; have gained new meaning as a result of COVID-19. According to a recent LIMRA poll, almost one-fourth of employers believe short-term disability and life insurance are more significant now than they were previously. In addition, over 40% felt that critical sickness and hospital indemnity coverage are more vital today than they were before the pandemic.

Benefits that may have previously positioned a company as an employer of choice may no longer be available. And not providing any perks is becoming a bigger barrier to attracting and retaining the talent required. Many business owners believe their firm is too small or that benefits are too expensive; however the majority of the companies we work with employ less than 100 people, and more than half employ fewer than 25.

Supplemental benefits, such as mental health benefits, are becoming increasingly important. With the prevalence of stress, anxiety, and depression on the rise, more employees are seeking to their employers for benefits that support both their physical and mental health. According to a survey conducted by the National Alliance of Healthcare Purchaser Coalitions, 53% of businesses are providing particular emotional and mental health programs for their employees as a result of the pandemic. According to the most recent data from Principal, 32% of companies have enhanced mental health and well-being benefits to meet the demand.

The impact of the epidemic on employees' personal finances is causing a lot of stress, which is boosting interest in financial wellness benefits. More businesses are emphasizing the need of assisting their employees in navigating financial issues, both individually and as a family, by providing benefits and resources that help them gain better financial control.

What role does financial pressure play in the evolution of benefits?

Open enrollment presents challenging decisions that may usher in an age where employers re-evaluate their benefits programs, with persistent financial uncertainty stressing bottom lines for small businesses across the country.

Employers recognize the importance of benefits like healthcare, and according to Principal research, have boosted the benefit by more than a quarter since March. Businesses that have been severely damaged by the pandemic, on the other hand, may be eager to pass on higher expenses. Employee premiums may rise as a result, and other benefits may be altered as a result.

As a result, we might witness a movement toward voluntary benefits. Employers, on the other hand, should be cautious about the potential consequences. Employee interest in purchasing 100 percent employee-paid products ranged from 35 percent for life insurance to 39 percent for critical illness coverage, according to LIMRA, with many employees undecided about enrolling.

Putting together a top-notch employee benefits package is a delicate balancing act. There's a lot to think about, including your budget, employee demands, and the perks you want to provide. Small businesses, on the other hand, who invest in benefits now, are not only benefitting their employees, but also presenting themselves as an employer of choice.

For small businesses, there is a way forward.

The thought of a major benefits change is daunting. Communication is the first and most critical step for small business owners in developing a benefits package that meets the changing demands of their employees.

Asking employees what is important to them is a straightforward way for organizations to determine what shifts to make and when to make them.

Employees issues, such as whether or not they can pay the mortgage or keep medical bills from stacking up, are frequently the focus of these discussions, rather than particular benefits like disability or life insurance.

It's a discussion that can help you get to the heart of your employees' present demands, as well as how they may have changed throughout COVID-19. Future benefit packages should be guided by these shifting goals. And these incentive packages will help the company attract and retain the people it needs to succeed.

Small Business Cons during the Pandemic

The impact of the pandemic differed by industry, as did survival tactics.

Economists are measuring the pulse of small business as the pandemic begins to fade. Small businesses employ roughly half of the workforce, generate two-thirds of net new jobs, and account for 44 percent of total economic activity in the United States, so their performance is critical.

Clutch conducted a study to determine the four most significant financial difficulties they would face in 2020:

Revenue. The biggest financial challenge for 31% of respondents was a drop in revenue. Revenue was down for 45% of enterprises with up to 10 employees.

Surprising costs. Unexpected company expenses posed the biggest problem for 11% of small enterprises.

Financial know-how. One in ten respondents stated their largest issue was a lack of skill or experience in managing corporate money.

Assets. For 8% of small enterprises, the largest difficulty was a lack of money.

Huckleberry, a small-business insurance provider, conducted a separate study to see how small businesses fared during the pandemic and what they expect in the following year. Unsurprisingly, it discovered that, while obstacles differed by industry, the most significant stumbling block was a lack of funds.

According to Huckleberry, "four out of ten small firms lacked the money or cash flow to conduct their enterprises in 2020."

28 percent of survey respondents said they were challenged by a lack of demand for their service or product. New COVID-related regulations were also difficult for 26% of respondents to follow.

Five significant findings emerged from the Huckleberry survey:

1. The impact differed depending on the industry. The worst-affected businesses were those that required in-person connections. Child childcare institutions suffered the worst of the damage. According to Huckleberry statistics, active insurance coverage in the daycare industry has decreased by 43%. In the meantime, policies in both the retail and fitness industries have decreased by more than 20%.

Due to the mandatory shutdown, restaurants and barbershops struggled to keep open during the pandemic. In both businesses, active insurance policies fell by more than 10%.

However, some industries, particularly those related to house care and improvement, performed well in 2020. The number of active policies in the plumbing and HVAC industry increased by about 50%, while flooring contractors, landscaping services, and carpentry enterprises all fared well.

2. Companies discovered new strategies to adapt. As mandatory closings spread across the country, every company that relied on personal connections went online if it could. Retailers, in particular, shifted to online sales, while fitness studios began offering sessions over the internet. Meanwhile, restaurants who were unable to accommodate diners inside their establishments implemented curbside pickup for their customers.

Providing a safe environment for customers was critical for those businesses that were able to stay open. Many small firms required masks, and the majority implemented strict sanitizing and cleaning procedures.

3. Expenses have been cut. During the epidemic, seven out of ten firms slashed their budgets:

Sixty-one percent of the respondents reduced their marketing and advertising budgets.

Payroll was cut by 41%, with many staff being laid off as a result.

Three out of ten people have reduced their rent or mortgage payments.

Nearly a quarter of respondents chose to go without company insurance. Seventy-seven percent of businesses that wanted to decrease insurance expenses did so by dropping their general liability policy, 62 percent by cutting their business owners policy, and 38 percent by focusing on workers' compensation and commercial auto insurance.

Vaccination will be required in many cases. Nearly a third of business owners indicated they will force their staff to acquire COVID-19 vaccines, while more than half said they will not. Others are undecided and will wait to see what happens in 2021.

4. A small number of people took advantage of government loans. Only 34% of small firms received government funds or loans, such as the Paycheck Protection Program, despite significant cash flow problems and cost reduction. In 2020, half of those polled were still profitable at the end of the year, while the other half broke even or lost money.

5. The business community is cautiously optimistic. The small-business community is enthusiastic about 2021, but there are conflicting feelings and no one is preparing too far ahead. Half of those polled indicated they were confident about running their company in 2021, while 29% said they were gloomy. The remaining 21% stated they were undecided about their chances.

How to achieve financial freedom with a successful small business

In the United States, owning and operating a small business is a trendy trend. According to a survey, the country has more than 28 million small enterprises, 22 million of which are self-employed and have no additional employees.

Many people regard financial independence to be one of the most important benefits of self-employment. However, not all small business entrepreneurs devote enough time and effort to planning for the future. According to BMO Wealth Management, three-quarters of small business owners had retirement savings of less than $100,000. Business financial demands frequently obstruct retirement savings. The good news is that there are savings choices, such as a self-directed Solo 401k plan, that can help them attain financial independence while allowing them to make their own investing selections.

How Can Your Small Business Help You Become Financially Independent?

You will always have numerous priorities competing for your financial resources as a small business owner. The trick is to create a plan that you can stick to.

Pay yourself first: Rather than paying yourself last, start paying yourself first, which means your retirement contributions, will be deducted first from your monthly income. Find out where you're wasting money and how to streamline your business to save money.

Set up a checking account that deducts a pre-determined amount from your business account on a regular basis. It will ensure that you have the money to make your annual contributions.

Set up a succession plan: While many small business owners talk about succession, only a small percentage of them have a strategy in place. Seek expert advice and bring on board people who can run your firm successfully long after you've retired. Your firm will be more appealing to a potential investor if you have a robust succession plan and management team in place.

Choose a Retirement Plan that Offers Investment Freedom

A Self-Directed Solo 401(k) Plan

If you own and operate a one-person firm, a self-directed Solo 401k is a great place to start. The presence of self-employment activity and the lack of full-time employees are the only requirements for starting a Solo 401k plan.

Contribution limits: In 2021, you can contribute up to $60,000, including a $6,000 catch-up contribution.

Optional investments include: You can invest in a variety of asset classes with a self-directed Solo 401k, including real estate, tax deeds/liens, precious metals, mortgage notes, private equity, personal loans, and even stock/bond investments.

Participant loan: Every eligible plan participant can borrow up to $50,000 or 50% of the plan balance, whichever is less. This cash can be used for anything, including paying off credit card debt, paying tuition, and even taking a trip.

Roth savings: There are no income limits on Roth Solo 401k retirement accounts. Regardless of your salary; you can contribute up to $24,000 every year.

Easy management: Self-directed Solo 401k plans with less than $250,000 in net assets are exempt from filing requirements, making them easier to handle.

As a small business owner, you have a huge possibility of having financial freedom in the future; all you have to do is get started and stay on track.

Resources

<u>Consulting for Lucky Breaks</u> – A successful entrepreneur helps others by sharing her skills and expertise.

<u>Google Drive</u> is a free alternative to Microsoft Office. (We prefer unrestricted) Plus, rather than having to open your Word or Excel documents using your computer's installed software, Google Drive is simply a click away. Any smartphone, tablet, or computer may access your files in Drive. As a result, your files will follow you wherever you go.

<u>Entrepreneurs on Fire</u> - This podcast features interviews with entrepreneurs just like you to help you achieve your goals.

<u>Google Calendar</u> is a free web-based calendaring service that allows you to keep track of all of your essential professional and personal activities in one location. You can share your schedule, work offline, and do a lot of other things. With Google Tasks, you can keep track of your daily to-do list, organize numerous lists, and track crucial deadlines. Create and update tasks from Gmail or Calendar; changes are automatically reflected in both places.

<u>Pocket</u> is a free tool that allows you to save links and articles in one location to read at a later date.

<u>Evernote</u> is an excellent program for jotting down your thoughts in the form of 'notes' for later reference.

The emphasis of <u>Squarespace</u> is on great design. A large image gallery, a logo creator, and much more are all included in your subscription. Squarespace, like others, allows you to sell online.

[Chargify](): If you're starting a subscription business and don't want to deal with the headache of creating a billing mechanism, [Chargify]() is a good option. They'll take care of the regular payments and give you the freedom to offer your clients a variety of subscription alternatives.

Chapter Three – Business Location – Brick and Mortar VS Online

Online stores are fantastic, but there are numerous reasons to prefer a brick-and-mortar business.

The internet has irrevocably altered our shopping habits. Many individuals use the internet to shop for clothing, groceries, and anything else they want or need. Is it, however, always the best option to go online? Though internet stores are convenient, there are many compelling reasons to visit a physical shop.

If you're thinking about starting a retail business, you should think about it thoroughly. When selecting whether to go online or offline, there are a few things to consider.

Humans have a long history of bartering and trading goods in exchange for one another. While the fundamentals have stayed constant throughout history – you give something in order to receive something – the mechanisms have changed over time. People have continued to engage in business in the hope of profit and success, from the agora of Ancient Greece to the modern supermarket, and from high-end boutiques to internet retailers.

If one were to divide today's business methods into two groups, they would be:

1. Brick and Mortar Businesses, and
2. Online Businesses

The Brick and Mortar Business

The traditional form of doing business- brick and mortar - may be quite costly and time consuming to set up. If the firm is to have any chance of flourishing, it is critical to secure a suitable site, and such valued properties are not cheap. Then there's the overhead, which includes things like taxes, utility expenses, inventory, and labor.

The Benefits:

- Perhaps the most significant advantage of a physical store over an online store is that it allows customers to physically touch, feel, and scrutinize a product before making a purchase choice.
- Scams abound on the internet, and many have taken advantage of these chances. As a result, a brick and mortar store may provide clients with peace of mind, a sense of trust, and dependability.
- Find the perfect location, preferably in a high-traffic area, and people may just walk into your store—and become customers - without ever having heard of your marketing initiatives.

The Negatives:

- As previously stated, the launch and overhead costs of a brick and mortar store are typically rather high.
- Once you've posted the 'Closed' sign, your shop is officially closed till the next day.

Online Businesses

It is relatively easy to set up a more current, graphic style of doing business. You'll still have to do a lot of the same things, including market research and promotional efforts, but the beginning and overhead expenditures will be far lower.

The Benefits:

- An internet store may and does stay open and ready for business 24 hours a day, seven days a week, 365 days a year.

- If you've managed to make the proper amount of noise in the correct areas, you'll be able to attract more customers to your small business than you could with a traditional store.

- There are no space restrictions and no sales representatives are required. If 50 consumers go into a brick and mortar location, you'll most likely run out of both. With an internet store, you may serve thousands of people at once.

The Negatives:

- The major disadvantage of an internet business, in comparison to a physical store, is that there is very little, if any, interaction with customers.

- Because you won't be confined by shelf space to showcase things in an internet business, it's surprisingly easy to get distracted. It is critical that you choose a specialization for your small business and stick to it.

Each of these options, both conventional and modern, has its own set of benefits and drawbacks. And, while you can argue about which one is superior till the end of time, they are both here to stay for the foreseeable future. If you can afford it, opening a physical store as well as an online store for your small business is the best approach to being successful.

So, what kind of business do you run? Regardless of which option you choose, you must execute your marketing strategy correctly. You'll still need to attend numerous networking events and generate leads for your company. The strategies remain the same, but the tactics change on a regular basis. To cultivate loyal customers, make sure you're using one of the finest CRM systems, such as LeadsHelper, to build a leads database and send targeted trackable marketing messages to your audience.

Internet Enterprise vs. Traditional Enterprise

I used to consider creating and operating a number of trading and consulting businesses, but after learning more about the benefits of internet enterprises, my ideas for making significant money in the future have shifted. I believe that once people learn about the internet's commercial miracles, they will experience a paradigm change that will render brick and store enterprises obsolete.

In comparison to a traditional brick and mortar firm, starting an internet business does not necessitate a large amount of capital. Forget about the high costs of commercial space leasing, furniture, and personnel that traditional brick-and-mortar enterprises necessitate. Working capital for an internet business is as simple as a PC with an internet connection. Consider how much money can be saved simply by making that distinction. Why not lower the expense of running the business to two or three figures instead of four to five, or even six? Unless further advertising costs are included, the cost of running an internet business will never be less than three figures.

In terms of Return on Assets, the profit created by an internet firm is always higher than that of a brick and mortar business. Similarly, internet business owners will always make more money than brick and mortar business owners. The reason for this is because brick and mortar business owners invest a significant amount of money to establish and manage their company in a specific location. Internet entrepreneurs, on the other hand, spend significantly less on startup and operational costs. What makes online businesses so profitable is their capacity to reach millions of clients globally via the internet, but brick-and-mortar firms can only reach and profit from customers in their immediate vicinity.

The Internet and brick-and-mortar businesses function and are regulated in distinct ways. Internet businesses operate in a virtual marketplace and can be monitored from anywhere with an internet connection, whereas brick and mortar firms are limited to a single physical location. What's noteworthy about internet businesses is that their owners may operate and oversee their firms from the comfort of their own homes or while on vacation, something that brick and mortar business owners cannot do.

As an internet entrepreneur, life would undoubtedly be a dream comes true because they are the only ones who can work from home or travel while making money, unlike brick and mortar entrepreneurs who are forever stuck in the same location and struggle to keep operating costs low in order to keep the business afloat.

Resources

eFulfillment Service - This service is inexpensive and interfaces with the marketplaces you may already be using (Etsy, eBay, etc).

Rakuten Super Logistics — as part of a larger corporation, Rakuten is able to provide value-added services that fulfillment-only businesses cannot.

Fulfillment.com is a service that caters to businesses that sell globally.

CensusViewer is a free program that lets you view U.S. Census data visually on a map or in data reports for cities, counties, and entire states.

Google Trends: Use Google Trends to see what people are looking for and how the volume of searches for significant topics has changed over time.

Look no farther than LivePlan if you need to design a business plan, create a budget, or anticipate your sales and cash flow.

Zoho One is an all-in-one operating system that keeps track of all aspects of a company's operations.

Chapter Four - Business Name Selection

Many local businesses are still named after their proprietors if you drive through any rural community. In some places, names like "Walker's Drugstore" and "Carl's Café" are still prominent, although naming your business after yourself isn't always the greatest option. Many rural American towns are stuck in time, part of a micro-economy with little room for expansion and, in many cases, on the decline. Most aspiring entrepreneurs do not intend to launch a company in this manner; hence most businesses should avoid naming their company after themselves.

There are a few instances where employing your own name is the most effective marketing strategy. Use your own name if you are a well-known specialist in your sector and buyers will be compelled to buy your product because of your name. For obvious reasons, artists such as clothing designers and painters use their own names, and clients have grown to recognize styles by the artists' names. Small construction companies are sometimes named after their founders, while most national and international startups are moving away from this practice. Doctors, lawyers, and accountants form businesses under their own names, but they rely on their good reputation to generate business. Consider finding a more detailed approach to identifying your endeavor if your business idea does not rely on your current reputation to thrive.

One disadvantage of utilizing your name as a business name is that it provides no information to potential customers about what you do. Anything from pencil top erasers to luxury yachts could be sold by "Smith, Inc." Even "Smith's Boats" isn't going to help you stand out from the crowd. Anything from small models to ocean liners might be sold by the company. Rivercraft boats, on the other hand, conjure up images of mid-sized, well-built boats intended for usage on rivers.

Choosing the proper name for your company is no longer as simple as it once was. Even 20 years ago, any name you liked could definitely be used, even if it was already taken by another company in a different field. Your alternatives have become much more constrained since the emergence of the internet. Every new business requires an internet presence, and having a domain name that matches your business name is the best chance. Finding a business you like that is also available online is getting harder with over 100 million domain names currently in use.

STEP 1: DEVELOPING A BUSINESS NAME:

So you've made your choice. You've come up with a brilliant concept. You're ready to quit your job and pursue your passion. You're just one step away from starting your own company. You're one step closer to being your own boss. You're one step closer to becoming an entrepreneur, but you still need to come up with a business name...

A company name is something that should never be taken lightly.

When choosing a name for your company, there are numerous factors to consider. Is the business local, national, or international, depending on what you want to do, where you want to do business, and what industry you want to get into? Is your company involved in the construction, manufacture, sale, purchase, trade, or distribution of something? Each of these criteria can have an impact on the name you choose. Is your company a non-profit? Is your company a member of a group? Is it a family-owned company?

I'd like you to acquire a piece of paper and a pen before I start going over some examples. Make a list of several names that would be appropriate for your company. Keep all of the names close together so you can compare them and go through them again and again.

Let's have a look at some of the samples that are impacted by the following statements:

Using your first and last names:

Real Estate is a service-based business (Ex. Lemieux Realtor) - Mortgage Consultant (The Lemieux Mortgage Group) - Legal Services (Lemieux Law Firm) - Martin's Design Concepts (design) - Composition (Lemieux Writing Services) - Business (Lemieux Enterprises) - Independent contractors (Lemieux Building Group) - Martin's Reno Services (renovators) - Printing services (Lemieux Print Shop)

Based on a product: - Pizza Joint (Martin's Pizza Delight) - Toys (Martin's Toy Shop) - Clothing (Lemieux Fashion) - Home equipment (Lemieux Appliances)

As you can see, all of these business name choices refer to two things: my name and what I do. The objective is to include your personal name and industry into your business name. It doesn't matter if you use your first or last name.

What is important is that you like your given name. A business name can live with you until you die, and it has the ability to be passed down through your family for generations.

Names with a twist:

These illustrations will be something I came up with on the spur of the moment to offer you some inspiration. Each name will be accompanied by a phrase that will explain what the name means.

Based on a service: - Online Promotion ("eMarket Promo" - Internet Marketing Promotion For Your Business) - Art Direction ("Crystal Graphics Firm" - Graphics that wow people) Clean Cut Barbers ("Clean Cut Barbers" - Haircuts that clean up your style) - Networking for Business ("NETeGroup" - Entrepreneurs Grouping For More Business Leads)

Hydraulic systems are based on a product ("ProHyd Systems" - Professional hydraulics that last). - Cues for the pool ("StickBall Cues" - A pool cue that sticks to its game) - Energy Bars ("SafeBars" - A power bar safe for the whole family)

A simple play on words, combined with brief descriptions of your product or service, can help you come up with something a little more original. Despite the fact that these names were produced in less than 10 minutes, take your time with them; you should never rush these things. A business name should never occur to you in a flash. Allow some time for the thoughts to develop. Even if you think you've found the perfect name, leave it alone and revisit it frequently. Inquire about your selections with friends, family, and coworkers.

Names of local businesses:

Locally based services should have a name that explains what they do. It should be straightforward and memorable. To illustrate what I mean, I'll use my own location (Hamilton, Ontario) in these cases.

- Lawn Care Across the City (Hamilton Lawn Care) - Real Estate - Mortgage Brokers (Hamilton Mortgage Group) (Greater-Hamilton Homes) - Job placement service (Hamilton Employers)

- Insurance Brokers - Insurance (Ontario Insurance Specialists) - Delivery of parcels (Ontario Mailing Systems) - Apple Farm (Ontario Apple Trees) - Movers (Relocators of Ontario)

- Baby Clothes - Baby (Canadian Baby Wear) - Personal computers (Computers Made in Canada) - Professional advisors (Canadian Consulting Group) - Printing services (PrintCanada)

For suggestions, it's a little easier to come up with a business name that targets your local area. Always make an effort to include your city, province/state, or country in the equation when describing the service region you provide. Make sure to look for other businesses with the same name on the internet. Because of how easy it can be for people to remember your name, many local businesses choose this way of selecting a wonderful name.

This finishes my suggestions for coming up with a business name. I still have a lot to teach you about naming, but it would take me to write a novel, and I want to cover all of the essentials in this tutorial, not just one.

STEP 2: SEARCH FOR DUPLICATE NAMES:

Once you've narrowed down your business name list to 1-5 options, it's time to perform some web research to see if anyone else has already stolen your name.

Everyone's online search experience will be unique. Depending on the type of business you wish to start, there are several approaches to look for duplicate business names.

When conducting an internet search, you must first determine:

1) Are you a local, provincial/state-wide, national, or worldwide business?

2) Will you register your name as a trademark or copyright? Also...

    A) Are there any other companies with the same name as you?

    B) Does one of your competitors own a trademark or copyright to a name that sounds similar to yours?

1.1) Geographical:

This is the one that is most likely to be found. You may usually run a search within Google/Yahoo/MSN with your business name in quotes, such as "My Term" in "My City", "Province/State", "Country" (for example, search for "Lawn Care Guys in Hamilton, Ontario, Canada") to check if exact results for that name are found. To achieve different results, try the same thing without the quotations. If you do obtain results, look through the website to discover if the results were "manufactured" by search engines for their own purposes, or if they are a true business name.

Don't forget to check the results to see if they match the type of business you want to start.

The industry in which you want to work has an impact on the availability of your name. For instance, you may call your company "Hamilton Lawn Maintenance." I promise that when you make a search, search engines will mix the words "Hamilton" and "Lawn" and "Maintenance" to construct their results. I'm sure there's a lawn maintenance service in Hamilton. Can you see how that might muddle your search results? Don't get disappointed if you find several matches while searching online; this is just the beginning.

1.2) Statewide / Provincial:

You'll want to search in the same way you did in "1.1) Local," but now you'll want to eliminate the "City" from your searches to see if you can locate a name that sounds similar to yours right away. If you get any results from your search, look into it further by visiting the website (s) you found.

If a possible competitor already has the name you desire, scratch it and forget about it. You don't want to end up in court later for something that may be avoided today.

1.3) National:

Same thing, but in your searches, only add your "Country."

1.4) International:

Simply look for your company name in "Quotes." Instead of using a country-specific search engine like Google.ca, conduct your queries on Google.com. Search engines will be able to provide you an accurate match for your business name if you include quotes. It won't matter if other companies use your name unless you're directly associated in the same industry and they possess the copyright to that name.

1.5) Copyright / Trademark:

"A trademark or trade mark is a distinctive symbol of some type that is used by an individual, business organization, or other legal entity to distinguish its products and/or services from those of other entities and to uniquely identify the source of its products and/or services to consumers." Wikipedia

When looking for a business name online, avoid names that are similar to a trademark. If you copy a trademark, you could face serious consequences, including a lawsuit. In fact, a gentleman on the internet has been debating this concept for quite some time. Nissan, a well-known automobile manufacturer, owns a trademark on its name and logo, but not on http://www.Nissan.com. They missed the deadline to purchase the domain name, and they are now suing the owner for ten million dollars in damages, a lawsuit that has been ongoing since 1999.

If you want to trademark your name, you must first ensure that no one else is using it. Phrases, words, logos, and images all fall within this category. The difficult aspect is rebranding an existing product. For example, you would have a lot of trouble trademarking "Business Name" in Canada because so many individuals already use the phrases "business name" and "business name" together online before you ever filed a trademark application.

I advise you to employ an expert to assist you with your trade marking requirements. This will provide you access to government databases that will allow you to browse through past trademarks and assist you in searching for other names that may prevent you from trademarking your name.

For some, trademarking is prohibitively expensive, but once you have one, no one else can use your good name for anything else without your express written consent. This was a mistake I made with my first company, "Smartads." People began to use smartads for their own objectives over time, some for good and some for harm.

STEP 3: CHECKING A GOVERNMENT DATABASE FOR TRADEMARKS

For the most part, you can conduct a business name search at your local business name register office.

Resources

Domain Name Generator - This clever application searches for the right domain name using synonyms, suffixes, prefixes, and more.

WordLab name generators - For you to consider, this keyword/sentence generator generates fully random choices.

Namelix - This website generates short, brand able names based on keywords you provide.

BNG - Business Name Generator generates millions of results based on your search queries.

Namesmith.io is a website where you can create a unique name. Namesmith.io is a more creative tool that includes both random and curated alternatives.

Wordoid - Users enter keywords on the left and are given names that start with, terminate with, or contain a fragment of the original inquiry.

To search for domain names, simply go to:

http://www.GoDaddy.com

https://www.namecheap.com

Chapter Five - Small Business Essentials

Starting a small business necessitates perseverance, motivation, and knowledge. So you've got some great ideas and a strong staff to help you make them a reality. Your modest startup business is unquestionably on its way to creating an impression.

However, you'll need a solid arsenal to achieve your objectives. You'll need gear and essentials to get the work done and move your startup forward in the direction you want it to go.

With that in mind, no matter what area of business you're in, there are vital cornerstones that no small business in today's world can thrive without:

How to Pick the Right Legal Structure for Your Business

Choosing the appropriate legal structure is an important aspect of running a company. It's critical to understand your alternatives, whether you're just starting out or your company is expanding.

Depending on the entity's finance and liability structure, partnerships can operate as either a sole proprietorship or a limited liability partnership.

If it cannot be established that members of an LLC engaged in an illegal, unethical, or negligent manner in carrying out the business's activities, they are immune from personal accountability for the debts of the company.

Corporations can sell stock to raise money for expansion, but sole proprietors can only get money from their personal bank accounts, personal credit, or taking on partners.

This paper is for business owners who want to learn more about the various legal structures for small businesses.

Analyzing your organization's goals and examining local, state, and federal laws are the first steps in determining the best legal structure for your company. You can choose the legal structure that best suits your company's culture by establishing your aims. You can adjust your legal form as your company expands to meet its new needs.

To assist you in deciding on the right legal structure for your company, we've developed a list of the most popular forms of business entities and their distinguishing characteristics.

Different kinds of business arrangements

Sole proprietorships, partnerships, limited liability companies, corporations, and cooperatives are the most frequent types of business entities. Here's more information on each legal framework.

1. Sole proprietorship

This is the most basic type of business structure. In a sole proprietorship, one person is solely liable for the profits and obligations of the business.

"A sole proprietorship allows you to be your own boss and manage a business from home without having to have a physical storefront," said Deborah Sweeney, CEO of

MyCorporation. "This company does not provide for the separation or protection of personal and professional assets, which could become a problem as your firm expands and more components of it hold you responsible."

The cost of a proprietorship varies depending on the market in which your company operates. State and federal fees, taxes, equipment demands, office space, banking costs, and any professional services your business decides to contract are all examples of early expenses. Freelance writers, tutors, bookkeepers, cleaning service providers, and babysitters are examples of these enterprises.

Some of the advantages of this business structure are as follows:

Setup is simple. The simplest legal structure to establish is a sole proprietorship. This may be the best business form for you if your company is solely owned by you. Because you have no partners or executive boards to answer to, there is relatively little paperwork.

The price is low. License fees and business taxes are the only fees involved with a proprietorship, and they vary based on which state you live in.

Deduction for taxes. You may be qualified for certain company tax deductions, such as a health insurance deduction, because you and your business are a single entity.

Exit is simple. Creating a sole proprietorship is simple, as is quitting one. You can disband your firm at any time as a sole proprietor with no official paperwork necessary. For example, if you open a daycare center and decide to close it down, you can simply stop operating it and advertise your services.

Examples of sole proprietorships: One of the most prevalent legal structures for small businesses is the sole proprietorship. Many well-known businesses began as sole proprietorships and developed into multibillion-dollar enterprises.

Here are a few examples:
- eBay
- JC Penny
- Walmart
- Marriott Hotels

2. Partnership

This business is owned by two or more people. A general partnership, in which all profits are shared equally, and a limited partnership, in which only one partner controls the business while the other person (or persons) contributes to and receives a portion of the profits, are the two varieties. Depending on the entity's finance and liability structure, partnerships can operate as either a sole proprietorship or a limited liability partnership (LLP).

"This entity is great for anyone who wants to start a business with a family member, friend, or business partner, such as a restaurant or an agency," Sweeney added. "Within the corporate structure, a partnership allows participants to share earnings and losses and make decisions jointly. Keep in mind that you will be held liable for your judgments as well as your business partner's behavior."

A general partnership can be more expensive than a sole proprietorship because you'll need an attorney to analyze your partnership agreement. The price range is influenced by the attorney's experience and region. For a general partnership to be effective, it must be a win-win situation for both parties.

Google is an example of this type of company. Larry Page and Sergey Brin co-founded Google in 1995 and grew it from a modest search engine to the world's most popular search engine. The co-founders met while earning their doctorates at Stanford University and later left to build a beta version of their search engine. They obtained $1 million in cash from investors shortly after, and Google began seeing thousands of visits every day. They have a combined net worth of nearly $46 billion as a result of their ownership of 16% of Google.

Here are a few of the benefits of forming a business partnership:

It's simple to make. There isn't as much paperwork to file as there is with a single proprietorship. If your state requires you to conduct business under a false name ("doing business as," or DBA), you'll need to obtain a Certificate of Conducting Business as Partners and write an Articles of Partnership agreement, both of which come with additional expenses. In most cases, a business license is also required.

Possibility of expansion. When there are multiple owners, you have a better chance of getting a company loan. If you have a bad credit score, bankers may consider two credit lines rather than one.

Taxation with a difference. General partnerships are required to file federal tax Form 1065 as well as state forms, but they rarely pay income tax. On their individual income tax forms, both partners disclose their joint income or loss. You and your friend are co-owners if you founded a bakery with a friend and organized the business as a general partnership. Each owner brings to the company a particular amount of knowledge and working capital, which might influence each partner's share of the company and contribution. Let's say you contributed the most seed capital to the company; it's possible that you'll be given a bigger share percentage, thereby making you the majority owner.

Examples of partnerships

Partnerships are one of the most frequent types of business formations, second only to sole proprietorships. Here are some examples of successful collaborations:

- Warner Brothers
- Hewlett Packard
- Microsoft
- Apple
- Ben & Jerry's
- Twitter

3. Limited Liability Corporation (LLC)

A limited liability corporation (LLC) is a hybrid entity that allows owners, partners, or shareholders to reduce their personal obligations while still reaping the tax and flexibility benefits of a partnership. If it cannot be established that members of an LLC engaged in an illegal, unethical, or negligent manner in carrying out the business's activities, they are shielded from personal accountability for the debts of the company.

"Limited liability companies were created to give business owners the liability protection that corporations have while allowing gains and losses to pass through to the owners as income on their personal tax returns," Brian Cairns, CEO of ProStrategix Consulting, explained. "LLCs can have one or more members, and revenues and losses do not have to be shared equally."

The state filing fee, which can range from $40 to $500 depending on the state, is included in the cost of incorporating an LLC. The state of New York, for example, charges a $200 registration fee and a $9 biennial cost for forming an LLC. You must also file a biannual statement with the New York State Department of State.

Despite the fact that small firms can form LLCs, some huge corporations do so. Anheuser-Busch Companies, one of the largest beer companies in the United States, is an example of an LLC.

Examples of limited liability companies (LLCs)

The LLC is commonly used by accounting, tax, and law firms, but it can also be used by other sorts of businesses.

Well-known examples include:

- Pepsi-Cola
- Sony
- Nike
- Hertz Rent-a-Car
- eBay
- IBM

4. Corporation

A corporation is treated by the law as a separate entity from its owners. It possesses legal rights independent of its owners, including the ability to sue and be sued, acquire and sell property, and sell ownership rights in the form of stocks. Fees for forming a corporation differ by state and charge category. The S corporation and C corporation costs in New York, for example, are $130, while the nonprofit fee is $75.

Companies can be classified as C corporations, S corporations, B corporations, closed corporations, or nonprofit corporations.

C corporations, which are owned by shareholders, are taxed separately. Morgan Chase & Co. is a C corporation that is a multinational investment bank and financial services holding business. Many larger organizations, such as Apple Inc., Bank of America, and Amazon, apply for C corporations because they allow an unlimited number of stockholders.

S corporations, like partnerships and LLCs, were created for small enterprises to avoid double taxation. Owners are also only covered for a limited amount of responsibility. Widgets Inc. is an example of a straightforward S corporation:

employee salaries are subject to FICA tax, but further profits distributed by the S corporation are not subject to additional FICA tax.

B corporations, often known as benefit corporations, are for-profit businesses that aim to have a beneficial social impact. The Body Shop has earned B corporation accreditation after demonstrating a long-term commitment to environmental and social causes. The Body Shop uses its presence to fight for long-term change on topics such as human trafficking, domestic abuse, climate change, deforestation, and cosmetic industry animal experimentation.

Closed corporations are not publicly traded and have minimal liability protection. They are typically operated by a few stockholders. Closed corporations, sometimes known as privately held firms, offer more flexibility than publicly traded corporations. Hobby Lobby is a privately held, family-owned company that operates as a closed corporation. Hobby Lobby equities aren't traded on the open market; instead, they've been allotted to family members.

On a public market, open corporations can be traded. Many well-known businesses, such as Microsoft and Ford Motor Company, operate as open organizations. Each entity has taken control of the business and is now open to investment from anyone.

Nonprofit organizations exist to assist others in some capacity, and they are rewarded with tax exemption. The Salvation Army, the American Heart Association, and the American Red Cross are examples of nonprofits. The main goal of these sorts of business arrangements is to focus on something other than making a profit.

The following are some of the benefits of this business structure:

Liability is limited. Stockholders are only accountable for their personal investments and are not personally liable for claims against your company.

Continuity. Death or the transfer of shares by shareholders has no effect on corporations. Investors, creditors, and customers prefer that your business continues to run indefinitely.

Capital. When your company is incorporated, it is considerably easier to raise huge amounts of money from various investors.

Rather than a startup based in a living room, this form of business is suitable for businesses that are farther along in their growth. For example, if you've founded a shoe company and have already given it a name, selected directors, and secured funds from investors, the next step is to incorporate. You're basically doing business at a higher-risk, higher-reward rate. Additionally, your company could file as a S corporation to take advantage of the tax benefits that come with it.

Corporations as examples;

It's probably in your best interest to incorporate your business once it reaches a particular size.

There are numerous well-known examples of corporations, such as:

- General Motors
- Amazon
- Exxon Mobil
- Domino's Pizza
- P. Morgan Chase

5. Cooperative

A cooperative (co-op) is a business that is owned and operated by the people it serves. Its services benefit the company's members, also known as user-owners, who vote on the mission and direction of the organization and share earnings. Cooperatives have the following benefits:

Reduced taxes. A cooperative, like an LLC, does not tax its members' earnings.

Funding has been increased. Federal grants may be available to help cooperatives get founded.

Discounts and improved service are available.

Cooperatives can make use of their scale to get discounts on goods and services for their members.

Choosing a business name that specifies whether the cooperative is a corporation, such as incorporated (Inc.) or limited, is a difficult task. The cost of registering a co-op agreement varies by state. The filing charge for an incorporated business in New York, for example, is $125.

CHS Inc., a Fortune 100 company owned by agricultural cooperatives in the United States, is an example of a co-op. CHS, the country's largest agribusiness cooperative, has recorded a net income of $829.9 million for the fiscal year that ended on August 31, 2019.

Cooperatives as examples

Co-ops, unlike other forms of enterprises, are owned by the individuals who use them.

Co-ops include the following notable examples:
- Land O'Lakes
- Navy Federal Credit Union
- Welch's
- REI
- Ace Hardware

The sole proprietorship, partnership, Limited Liability Company, corporation, and cooperative are the five forms of business structures. The structure you choose is largely determined by the nature of your firm. You'll be able to change structures as your company expands to fit its needs.

Consider these factors before deciding on a business structure.

It's not always straightforward to pick which structure to use for new enterprises that fall into two or more of these categories. You should think about your startup's financial demands, risk, and growth potential. It can be tough to change your legal structure after you've registered your company, so think about it carefully when you're first starting out.

Here are some crucial things to think about while deciding on a legal structure for your company. You should also schedule a meeting with your CPA to seek his or her counsel.

Flexibility

Where do you see your company going, and what kind of legal structure will allow it to expand the way you want it to? Review your goals in your business strategy and choose which structure best suits those aims. Your organization should foster the prospect of development and change rather than stifle it.

Complexity

Nothing beats a sole proprietorship when it comes to starting and operational complexity. You simply register your business name, begin doing business, record your profits, and pay personal income taxes on it. Outside funding, on the other hand, can be difficult to come by. Partnerships, on the other hand, necessitate a formal agreement that spells out the duties and profit splits. State governments and the federal government have different reporting obligations for corporations and limited liability companies.

Liability

Because it is its own legal entity, a corporation carries the least level of personal culpability. This means that creditors and consumers can sue the company, but they won't be able to seize the officials' or shareholders' personal assets. An LLC provides the same level of protection as a sole proprietorship while also providing tax benefits. Partnerships divide liabilities among the partners according to the terms of their partnership agreement.

Taxation

An LLC owner pays taxes in the same way that a sole proprietor does: all profits are treated as personal income and taxed as such at the end of the year.

"You want to avoid double taxes as a small business owner in the early stages," Jennifer Friedman, chief marketing expert at Expertly.com, stated. "The LLC structure prohibits this and ensures that you are taxed as an individual rather than a corporation."

Individuals who are part of a partnership can claim their share of the profits as personal income as well. To minimize the end effect on your return, your accountant may recommend quarterly or biannual advance payments.

Each year, a corporation files its own tax returns, paying taxes on profits after deducting expenses such as wages. If you receive compensation from the corporation, you must pay personal taxes on your personal return, such as Social Security and Medicare.

Control

A sole proprietorship or an LLC may be the best option for you if you want sole or principal control over your business and its activities. Control can also be negotiated in a cooperation agreement.

A corporation is designed to have a board of directors that makes the company's important decisions. A single individual can oversee a corporation, especially at its birth, but as it grows, the requirement for it to be run by a board of directors grows as well. The regulations designed for larger companies – such as keeping track of every key action that affects the company – nevertheless apply to small businesses.

Investment in capital

If you need outside finance, such as from an investor, venture capitalist, or bank, forming a corporation may be a preferable option. Corporations are more likely than sole proprietorships to be able to seek outside finance.

Corporations can sell stock to raise money for expansion, but sole proprietors can only get money from their own accounts, personal credit, or by bringing in partners. An LLC can suffer comparable challenges, albeit because it is its own business, the owner does not always need to use their own credit or assets.

Regulations, licenses, and permits

You may require particular licenses and permits to operate in addition to officially registering your business entity. Depending on the sort of business and its activity, local, state, and federal licenses may be required.

Friedman explained that "states have various criteria for different company models." "There may be varying restrictions at the municipal level depending on where you start your shop. Understand the state and industry you're in when you choose your structure. It isn't a 'one-size-fits-all' solution, and firms may be unaware of what is relevant to them."

Only for-profit businesses are covered by the structures outlined here. Friedman recommends contacting a business law consultant if you've done your studies and still aren't sure which business structure is best for you.

Essentials tools for Small Businesses

Small businesses, or SMEs, must, nevertheless, make use of the technologies available to guarantee that their operations are streamlined. These are:

- Social Media Platforms
- Business email
- Business Phone
- Business Zoom
- Business Bank Accounts

Resources

Burst — this free photo site, powered by Spotify, has hundreds of images for commercial and personal use.

Shutterstock - Shutter stock is the most comprehensive option, selling photographs, images, videos, and music.

Pexels – These royalty-free and attribution-free pictures can be used anywhere.

One of our favorite online image editors is Canva. You can quickly edit images, but you can also create a wide range of visuals, including posters, business cards, and book covers. The basic version is free, and if you require more features, you may upgrade to the "work" edition.

Kickstarter is a United States-based global crowdsourcing website. The company's stated aim is to assist in the realization of creative ideas. Kickstarter funding is all-or-nothing. A pledge to a project will not be charged until it reaches its financing target.

Maestro Label Designer — this free web-based tool provides label users with customized design and printing possibilities.

The Print Shop - This CD program, which is a small business partner, will help you develop brochures, labels, newsletters, and more.

Chapter six - Business Plan the Secret Weapon!

Planning for business success

When you're running a business, it's easy to get caught up in the details and lose sight of the greater picture. Successful businesses, on the other hand, devote effort to developing and managing budgets, preparing and reviewing company plans, and routinely monitoring finances and performance.

Structured planning can make all the difference in your company's growth. It will allow you to focus your efforts on boosting earnings, lowering costs, and enhancing returns on investment.

Many organizations, in reality, carry out the majority of the activities connected with business planning, such as thinking about growth areas, competition, cash flow, and profit, even if they don't have a formal process in place.

It doesn't have to be complicated or time-consuming to turn this into a unified method for managing your company's growth. The most important thing is that plans are developed, that they are dynamic, and that everyone involved is aware of them. See the page on what to include in your annual plan in this handbook.

The advantages

The main advantage of business planning is that it allows you to focus on the path of your company and sets goals that will help it expand. It will also allow you to take a step back and assess your performance as well as the issues affecting your business. Business planning can provide you with the following benefits:

- A better ability to make continuous improvements and foresee issues.
- Dependable financial data on which to make decisions.
- Enhanced attention and clarity
- A boost in your decision-making confidence

Budgeting and planning in business:

The effectiveness of a business owner's planning process is critical to the success of a small firm. Business budget planning, which is also one of the final stages of the planning process, is one of the most important components of the planning process. To begin, gather financial data, predictions, and industry analysis to aid in the development of your business budget.

It's critical to plan and closely manage your company's financial success after it's up and running. The most effective approach to keeping your firm--and its money - on track is to establish a budgeting procedure.

This section describes how to plan and budget for your business and the benefits of doing so. It includes action items to assist you better manage your company's finances and make sure your plans are feasible.

Budgeting and strategic planning

Small business owners who are just starting out may not realize the importance of budgeting. You will, however, need to fund your plans if you are planning for the future of your company. Budgeting is the most effective strategy to keep track of your financial flow and invest in new prospects when the timing is right.

You may not always be able to be hands-on with every aspect of your business as it grows. You may need to divide your budget among many departments, such as sales, production, and marketing. You'll notice that money starts to flow in a variety of places throughout your company; budgets are a critical tool for staying in control of spending.

A budget is a strategy for:

- Keep financial control
- Make sure you'll be able to meet your current obligations.
- This empowers you to make sound financial decisions and achieve your goals.
- Ensure that you have sufficient funds for future projects.

It lays out how you plan to spend your money and how you plan to pay for it. It is not, however, a prediction. A forecast is a prediction of the future, whereas a budget is a planned outcome of the future, determined by your business strategy.

The advantages of a business budget

Drawing up a business budget has a lot of advantages, including being better prepared to:

- Efficiently handle your **finances**
- Projects should be given adequate resources.
- Keep an eye on things.
- You achieve your goals.
- Better decision-making
- Identify issues before they arise, such as the need for more funding or cash flow issues.
- Make a future plan
- Boost employee motivation.

Making a financial plan

The ability to create, monitor, and manage a budget is critical to a company's success. It should assist you in allocating resources where they are needed to keep your company profitable and successful. It doesn't have to be difficult. All you have to do now is figure out how much money you'll make and how much money you'll spend over the budget period.

What exactly is business capital, and why is it so crucial?

Business capital is an accounting phrase that you may not hear much about, but it could be the key to your company's success. Business capital has an impact on many elements of your organization, including paying staff and vendors, keeping the lights on, and planning for long-term growth. In a nutshell, working capital is the cash on hand to cover immediate, short-term obligations.

To make sure your business capital is working for you, you'll need to figure out what you have now, anticipate what you'll need in the future, and think about how to make sure you always have enough cash.

What is the formula for business capital?

Determine your working capital ratio, a gauge of your company's short-term financial health, to get a sense of where you are right now.

The formula for calculating business capital:

Current assets / current liabilities = working capital ratio.

Your working capital ratio is 2:1 if you have $1 million in current assets and $500,000 in current liabilities. Although a ratio of 1.2:1 is generally considered healthy, in some industries or types of enterprises, a ratio as low as 1.2:1 may be sufficient.

Your net working capital indicates how much cash you have on hand to cover current expenses.

The formula for net business capital:

Net working capital equals current assets less current liabilities.

Only short-term assets such as cash in your business account, accounts receivable (money owed to you by customers), and inventory that you anticipate to convert to cash within 12 months are considered in these calculations.

Accounts payable, which is money you owe vendors and other creditors, as well as other obligations and accumulated expenses for payroll, taxes, and other outlays, are all examples of short-term liabilities.

Recognizing your requirements

Plotting month-by-month inflows and outflows for your firm will help you get a better grasp of your working capital requirements. For example, a landscaping company's revenues may peak in the spring, then remain pretty stable through October, before plummeting to nearly zero in the late fall and winter. On the other hand, the company may have a large number of ongoing expenses throughout the year.

Parts of these computations may necessitate making educated estimates about what will happen in the future. While historical results might help, you'll also need to account for future contracts you plan to sign and the potential loss of key customers. Making accurate estimates might be especially difficult if your company is rapidly expanding.

These estimates can help you figure out which months have more money going out than coming in, and which months have the largest cash flow gap.

There are four reasons why your business could need more operating capital.

Seasonal variations in cash flow are common in many firms, which may require additional capital to prepare for a busy season or to keep the business running when revenue is low.

While waiting for payments from clients, almost every business will require additional working capital to meet obligations to suppliers, employees, and the government.

Extra working cash can benefit your business in a variety of ways, such as allowing you to take advantage of supplier discounts by purchasing in quantity.

Working capital can also be used to pay for temporary workers or other project-related costs.

Looking for ways to increase your business capital?

An unsecured revolving line of credit can be a good way to boost your operating capital. Lines of credit are meant to support temporary working capital needs, have better terms than business credit cards, and allow your company to draw only what it needs when it needs it.

While a company credit card can be a convenient way for you and your top employees to handle incidental expenses such as travel, entertainment, and other necessities, it is rarely the greatest answer for working capital. Increased interest rates, higher costs for cash advances, and the ease with which one might accumulate excessive debt are all limitations.

Obtaining a line of credit for business capital

Lenders will assess the overall health of your balance sheet, including your working capital ratio, net working capital, annual revenue, and other indicators when you apply for a line of credit. See what banks are looking for in businesses that are looking for funding.

Lenders will look at your personal financial accounts, credit score, and tax returns because small company owners' business and personal affairs are often connected. A personal guarantee of repayment will be required.

Although a variety of factors influence the size of your working capital line of credit, a general rule of thumb is that it should not exceed 10% of your company's revenues.

What is the significance of business accounting?

Accounting is critical for small business owners because it allows owners, managers, investors, and other stakeholders to assess the company's financial success. Accounting provides crucial information about costs and profits, profit and loss, liabilities and assets for decision-making, planning, and control activities inside a company.

Accounting's basic goal is to record financial transactions in books of accounts in order to identify, quantify, and transmit economic data. Furthermore, tax reporting companies need you to keep basic books that document income and expenses.

What Is the Importance of Accounting?

Accounting is essential to running a business because it allows you to track income and expenses, maintain statutory compliance, and offer quantifiable financial information to investors, management, and the government that can be used to make business choices.

Your records generate three important financial statements.

The income statement tells you how much money you made and how much money you lost.

The balance sheet gives you a clear view of your company's financial situation on a specific day.

The cash flow statement is a link between the income statement and the balance sheet that shows how much money was made and spent over a period of time.

If you want to keep your business afloat, you must keep your financial records clean and up to date. Here are a few of the reasons why it is critical for your company, no matter how big or little!

It aids in the evaluation of business performance.

Your financial records represent the financial situation of your small business or corporation as well as the results of operations. In other words, they assist you in gaining a better understanding of your company's financial situation. Clean and current records will not only help you keep track of spending, gross margin, and potential debt, but they will also allow you to compare current data to past accounting records and allocate your budget accordingly.

It ensures that the law is followed.

Although state laws and regulations differ, efficient accounting systems and processes will assist you in ensuring statutory compliance in your organization.

Liabilities such as sales tax, VAT, income tax, and pension funds, to name a few, will be treated effectively by the accounting department.

It assists in the creation of budgets and future projections.

Budgeting and future estimates can make or break a company, and your financial records will be critical in this regard.

To keep your operations profitable, business trends and estimates are based on previous financial data. This financial data is most useful when it comes from well-organized accounting operations.

It aids in the preparation of financial statements.

The Registrar of Companies requires businesses to file their financial statements. Listed companies must submit them to stock exchanges as well as to the IRS for direct and indirect tax purposes. Accounting, of course, plays a crucial part in all of these instances.

The Importance of Filing a Business Income Tax Return

Your success in life is measured in numbers: the numbers in your bank account and the annual profits reported on your tax return. These figures can either open or close doors, providing opportunities for progress and growth. By filing their annual income tax return, business owners and professionals will receive extra opportunities. Filing your income tax return has two purposes: it not only allows you to declare your earnings to the IRS and pay any taxes owed, but it also allows you to take advantage of various perks that will benefit you in the short and long term. Let's take a look at the advantages of filing your taxes as a business owner or professional.

Filing a Tax Return Has Many Advantages for Businesses and Professionals

Losses are carried forward.

Losses are unavoidable in the corporate world. If you have capital losses, you can deduct them from your income under the category "Profit and Gains of Business and Profession."

You can carry over your losses for up to 8 years if you file an income tax return. This option to carry forward losses, however, is only available if your annual tax return is filed. This implies you can carry over past losses to offset future gains in succeeding years to minimize the amount of taxes you owe.

Request a loan

Businesses, like individuals, require loans at various times in their lives. Loans are commonly used by businesses to expand and enhance their operations. When requesting for a loan at a critical stage in your organization's growth, your income tax return is a vital document that banks will want, among other things, before assessing if your business is a sound investment for them to award a substantial quantity of money that you should be able to repay. So, completing your income tax return on time, every year, provides benefits that will benefit you in several aspects of building your business.

Avoids Punishment and Prosecution

Tax evasion is punishable severely all around the world, especially in India. Late filing also comes with fines, which might eat into your profits. As a result, timely filing of your income tax returns will spare you from avoidable tough situations with the IRS, allowing you to focus on your business in peace.

Obtain Tenders from the Government

Your business's financial situation and achievements are reflected in your income tax returns. The successful verification of your financial records, which is done by verifying your annual tax returns for the last many years, is typically linked to the acquisition of government tenders. Cross-checking will be done on the applicant who is most suited for the tender to see if he or she is capable of overseeing the project. Professionals who want to land contracts should make sure their business tax returns are completed on time and precisely, as an audit may be required, just as it is for enterprises.

Depreciation Claim

According to income tax legislation, assets in the name of the firm or owner allow you to claim depreciation. The asset being claimed, however, must be used solely for the purposes of the business or profession. If you haven't chosen the Presumptive Taxation Scheme, you can compute your total taxable earnings by subtracting all expenses and depreciation allowed under section 32 of the income tax act. As a result, by preparing your tax returns, you may optimize your profits by taking advantage of all available deductions, such as depreciation.

Take advantage of the Presumptive Taxation Scheme.

Under the Presumptive Taxation Scheme under section 44AD, the Income Tax Department permits small enterprises and professionals to pay tax on only a percentage of their earnings, easing the burden of paying taxes. This scheme is available to professionals earning less than Rs 50 lakh and enterprises generating less than Rs 2 crore. Professionals are only required to pay taxes on 50% of their profits, whereas corporations are only required to pay taxes on 8% of their earnings. To take advantage of the benefits of this program, taxpayers must file ITR 4 tax returns.

Every person's ambition is to develop and grow. This expansion extends into the careers of enterprises and professionals. Filing your tax return on time each year can open doors to help you realize your ambitions of success and prosperity.

The Importance of POS (Point-of-Sale) Systems for Small Businesses

Today, POS systems are becoming more popular, and here are the top six reasons why shops choose to invest in one:

1. Sales Reports

A POS system provides you with a comprehensive view of your company and automatically tracks its cash flow. It is simple to find information about a product line.

Another advantage of a POS system is the ability to save information about your financial situation, inventory situation, and sales situation. You can plan the revenue that would be statistically expected for the month, the next two months, or the coming week based on this information.

Fill out the form on this page for a personal consultation on the best POS system for your business, and we will contact you. Our service is provided without charge.

2. Change Product Offers

Advanced reports can clearly show which product categories are the most profitable and which are the least profitable. Knowing which departments and items are underperforming might help you design a sales plan. As a result, based on your industry, you can adapt your store items, menu, and much more.

In addition, the system generates in-depth analysis of customers' purchasing habits on its own. This POS system feature will enable your organization to adjust to the needs of the group without the need for costly hours of research.

3. Save time

Another advantage of a POS system is that it allows you to keep track of deliveries and all goods leaving your store. The system keeps track of how much a certain product has sold and keeps you up to date on what you have in stock. When the inventory is nearly depleted, the POS system can submit orders to the suppliers on its own. As a result, there is no need for an employee to devote time to it.

When a buyer requests information on a certain product, the seller can immediately look it up in the program. Reducing the amount of time a customer has to wait will improve the level of service you can provide.

A POS system can also assist you with automatically defining margins and calculating taxes. Everyday chores for your staff will become easier and faster, whether they use stationary or mobile POS systems.

4. Reduce errors as much as possible

A product's price can be adjusted, and it will be updated throughout the system, ensuring that prices remain consistent throughout the process. As a result, the corporation ensures that prices always match the price quoted to the consumer in order to avoid unsatisfied customers.

5. Customer Loyalty Program

A POS system can save all of your customer information, allowing you to provide outstanding customer care to your loyal customers. In fact, it enables you to determine which of your consumers' favorite products are. When you customize your product offers and promotions for each of your consumers, this feature of POS systems can be really handy. They will feel special and well cared for, which may lead to a purchasing decision.

6. Management of Employees

A point-of-sale system can be used to track each employee's additional sales. It can, however, be utilized as a management tool and a reward criterion. Employees will be more motivated and effective as a result of this. As a result, revenues will rise and customer service will improve.

On the other side, the employee can review his or her own sales figures, which can aid in the employee's understanding of his or her own personal goals. It also allows them to see where they can enhance the numbers.

To recap, a POS system helps your firm become more cost-conscious, provides you a better understanding of revenues, saves time, enhances client relations, and uses previously collected data to develop economic targets.

Resources

Quickbooks produced this sales tax rates tool to assist small business owners in determining the appropriate sales tax rates. Your tax calculator will do it for you for free if you use Quickbooks or TurboTax.

SalesForce — with practically everything integrated, Sales Force is able to give intelligent reporting.

Quickbooks — this software can generate basic and custom reports, giving you a complete picture of your company.

Pipedrive — rather than waiting for reports, see your sales in real time with Pipedrive.

Monday.com - this organizational tool allows you to track your business in a customizable method.

Zendesk Sell — with sales forecasting tools and prediction capabilities, the future is now.

MailChimp Marketing CRM — this all-in-one marketing tool may assist you in gathering data, organizing it, and even automating some of your tasks.

Chapter Seven - Understanding Your Industry Competitors

Understanding your competition is critical to every company's success. Even if your product or service fills a niche in the market, there are always other companies that offer something similar, or various ways to meet the same customer's needs. When considering your competition, the goal is to understand why customers choose one product or service over another.

It's dangerous to expand your business without first learning about your competitors. Market research can help you prepare for shifting marketplaces and keep your company from falling behind the competition.

How to Conduct a Market Analysis for Your Business

A market analysis can help you figure out how to improve your company's competitiveness and customer service.

A market analysis is a comprehensive examination of a market within a particular industry.

Conducting a market analysis has a number of advantages, including lowering risk and better informing business decisions.

A market study can be broken down into seven steps.

This content is intended for business owners who want to learn why and how to perform a market study.

One of the first stages of business success is to understand your customer base. Your business may struggle to come up with a successful marketing strategy if you don't know who your clients are, what they want, and how they want to acquire it from you. This is where a market study comes into play. A market analysis can be a time-consuming task, but it can be completed in seven simple stages on your own.

What is the definition of a market analysis?

A market analysis is a comprehensive examination of a market within a particular industry. You will examine the dynamics of your market, such as volume and value, possible client categories, buying patterns, competition, and other crucial elements, using this analysis. The following questions should be answered by a thorough marketing analysis:

Who are the people who might be interested in doing business with me?

What are the purchase habits of my customers?

What is the size of my target market?

What is the maximum price my customers are willing to pay for my product?

What are my primary rivals?

What are the advantages and disadvantages of my competitors?

The main point to remember is that a market study is a complete examination of a market within an industry.

What are the advantages of conducting a marketing study?

A marketing study can help you manage risk, spot developing trends, and forecast income. You may utilize a marketing analysis at various stages of your business, and it's even a good idea to do one once a year to stay on top of any important market changes.

A thorough market study is frequently included in a business plan since it helps you gain a better understanding of your target audience and competitors, allowing you to develop a more targeted marketing approach.

Other significant advantages of completing a market analysis include:

Risk reduction: Knowing your market may help you decrease business risks since you'll have a better awareness of important market trends, key industry players, and what it takes to succeed, all of which will inform your business decisions. You can also undertake a SWOT analysis to assist in safeguarding your company further. A SWOT analysis evaluates a company's strengths, weaknesses, opportunities, and threats.

Targeted products or services: When you know exactly what your customers want from you, you'll be in a far better position to serve them. You may utilize this information to adjust your business's offerings to your consumers' demands once you know who they are.

Emerging trends: Being the first to discover a new opportunity or trend is a key part of staying ahead in business, and employing a marketing analysis to remain on top of industry trends is a wonderful way to position yourself to take advantage of this knowledge.

Market forecasts: A market prediction is an important part of most marketing assessments since it predicts future numbers, attributes, and trends in your target market. This provides you an estimate of how much money you'll make, allowing you to change your company plan and budget accordingly.

Benchmarks for evaluation: Measuring your company's success outside of basic numbers might be tough. A market study gives standards against which your firm can be judged and how well it is performing in comparison to others in your sector.

Marketing analytics can provide context for prior blunders and industry abnormalities in your company. In-depth analytics, for example, can explain what factors influenced a product's sale or why a certain statistic performed the way it did. Because you'll be able to examine and define what went wrong and why, you'll be able to prevent repeating the same mistakes or encountering similar anomalies in the future.

Marketing optimization: An annual marketing study may help you with this because it can guide your continuing marketing efforts and show you which elements of your marketing require improvement and which are functioning well in comparison to other companies in your sector.

The key message is that a market study may help your organization in a variety of ways, especially if you do them on a frequent basis to ensure you have up-to-date data for your marketing efforts.

What is the best way to perform a market analysis?

While doing a marketing study is not a difficult task, it does necessitate extensive research, so plan on devoting a significant amount of time to it.

The seven steps of doing a market analysis are as follows:

1. Set a goal for yourself.

You may be performing a market analysis for a variety of reasons, including gauging your competitors or learning about a new industry. Whatever your motivation is, it's critical to figure it out as soon as possible in order to stay on track throughout the process. Begin by determining whether your goal is internal – such as increasing cash flow or enhancing business operations – or external, such as obtaining a business loan. The type and amount of research you conduct will be determined by your goal.

2. Research the current state of the industry.

It's critical to offer a clear overview of your industry's present situation. Include where the industry appears to be headed, utilizing measures like size, trends, and predicted growth, as well as plenty of facts to back up your conclusions. You can also do a comparative market analysis to figure out where you have a competitive advantage in your market.

3. Figure out who your ideal customers are.

It would be a waste of effort to attempt to get everyone interested in your product, and it would be a waste of time to try to get everyone interested in your product. Instead, conduct target market research to determine who is most likely to want your product and concentrate your efforts there. You want to know how big your market is, who your consumers are, where they're located, and what factors might impact their purchasing decisions, such as:

- Age
- Gender
- Location
- Occupation
- Education
- Needs
- Interests

During your study, consider building a customer profile or persona that represents your ideal consumer and will serve as a model for your marketing efforts.

4. Understand who your competitors are.

To be successful, you must have a thorough grasp of your competitors' market saturation, what they do differently from you, and their strengths, limitations, and market advantages. Begin by making a list of all of your major rivals, then go through the list and perform a SWOT analysis on each one. What distinguishes that company from you? What makes a customer choose their company over yours? Put yourself in the shoes of the customer.

Then, from most to least dangerous, prioritize your list of competitors and set a schedule for doing regular SWOT analysis on your most dangerous competitors.

5. Gather additional information.

Information is your friend when it comes to marketing analysis; you can never have too much data. It's critical that the data you use is reliable and accurate, so be selective about where you receive your figures. Here are a few trustworthy business data sources:

- U.S. Bureau of Labor Statistics
- U.S. Census Bureau
- State and local commerce sites
- Journals of trade
- SWOT analysis of your own
- Questionnaires or market research

6. Analyze the data you've gathered.

After you've gathered all of the data you can and double-checked that it's accurate, you'll need to analyze it to make it helpful to you. Organize your research into parts that make sense to you, but be sure to include divisions for your goal, target market, and competitors.

Resources

Authorize.Net — this platform is well-known in the merchant services market as one of the leading gateway providers.

PayPal — Similar to Amazon, you can include a PayPal button in your checkout process to allow customers to use a payment processor they are familiar with.

Stripe — this payment processor is well-known for its versatility, allowing you to collect payments in-store, on mobile, online, and via invoices.

Each social media network has its own strategy for acquiring potential customers. Facebook, Twitter, and Instagram are just a few of the most basic and popular.

SEMRush is one of the most popular SEO tools on the market, but its competitor analysis capabilities set it apart from the competition.

Sprout Social allows you to analyze competitor social media performance from a variety of perspectives and data sources. With numerous data points you can track across Facebook, Twitter, and Instagram, you can utilize Sprout's array of competitive analyses to review and optimize your social strategy.

Ahrefs - One of the most widely used paid marketing tools in the world; Ahrefs can analyze your domain, product pages, articles, and more.

Conclusion

Now is the moment to put your business idea to the test, which means you must concentrate on producing some sales. Profitability is, after all, the yardstick by which successful enterprises are judged.

There is no perfect plan for starting a business, and you may make a lot of mistakes in the beginning. Partnering with more established businesses can help you get your name out there and expand faster.

You should be prepared to change your strategy as you go, regardless of whatever one you choose. The most crucial thing is that you provide a solution that is relevant to your clients and meets a need.

www.ingramcontent.com/pod-product-compliance
Lightning Source LLC
Chambersburg PA
CBHW070325100426
42743CB00011B/2558